Myra Brooks-Turner Piano Duet Collection

The Flamingo Waltz

(1 Piano - 4 Hands)

71-12

The Flamingo Waltz

To Stacy, Cheryl and Terri

Myra Brooks-Turner, Op. 63 No. 83

Schaum Publications, Inc.
10235 N. Port Washington Rd.
Mequon, WI 53092
www.schaumpiano.net

Level Six

ISBN 978-1-62906-014-9

EXCLUSIVELY
DISTRIBUTED BY
HAL LEONARD

00645842
U.S. $3.99   7112